*Do This and Never Be Lost in
Your Business Direction Again.
By Stefan N. Chapman*

Foreword

Thank you for taking the time to invest in yourself, your business and in me by purchasing this booklet. When I began my very first business venture, I was very lost and had no clue about how to begin. I just knew that I wanted to start my own business. No one was around to mentor and guide me through the process, from start to finish. However, I'm very persistent and I knew that I had time.

At the time there was no internet; at least not like it is today, so I had to research the old fashioned way. I hung around businessmen, shop owners and the library. I read every book that I could. Ultimately, I just got up and started the process. When someone told me that I couldn't do something, I didn't argue. I simply complied, and then politely asked them how I should go about doing it. It was through trial and error, and countless failures and setbacks that I finally stumbled across the way that I'm about to share with you.

Although things times have changed a bit, and technology has improved; the process still remains very much the same. In an effort to be totally transparent, this booklet is intended for the beginner business owner who has never owned their own business, but have always wanted to. Maybe your were afraid of failing or simply afraid of the unknown. This is the time where you have to decide if you are going to continue planning, or start doing.

Your Passion

It's an old cliche, but it still holds true. Do what you're passionate about. Some would argue that your passion might not pay the bills. I beg to differ with that. In today's era, with the knowledge that we as a people have accumulated, your business is only limited by the confines of your imagination.

It really is true that you can do anything that you set your mind to do. The problem is that many people will tell you that you can't do it. They do this because they have cast their own fears, shame and doubt onto you because they were unable to accomplish their dreams. With all due respect to them; find yourself a new set of friends to hang around with. It's like the saying; "birds of a feather, flock together". Like-minded people tend to hang out with one another. If your friends are complainers, doubters, negative and pessimistic; then you will be negative and pessimistic as well. This is why the rich only associate with the rich. Money attracts money.

I don't mean to be insensitive, mean or cruel but I'm very positive. I believe that I can do anything. This is why I don't share my dreams with everyone. I only share my dreams with people who are for me, who will support my vision and cheer me on. This is not about my ego. It's about knowing who I am. If someone in my company tells me; "you can't do it, that's too hard or is a complainer". I'm very polite, but I will begin distancing myself away from them. When I see them, I will be polite, but their negativity has no place in my destiny.

What's your passion? Your passion should be what you are gifted at. Some would say that they don't know what their gift is. Quite simply, your gift is whatever you do that comes easy to you, that you can do on a daily basis. If you think about it, you already know what your gift is. Now you just have to turn it into a business.

My gift is motivating people and sharing my experiences and knowledge. I've learned the hard way how to begin and run a business. Now I'm very excited to motivate you and share with you how to start your own.

The Business Plan

Let's jump right in with the nuts and bolts; the business plan. The number one item that held true for me was to begin with a business plan. Some of you may say that you don't need a business plan because you know what you want to accomplish. Do you have funding? Will you require capital from a lender or a bank for your business? If now, then you had better begin with a business plan.

A business plan will spell out very plainly your business for investors and banks. They want to know two things. First, why should they loan their money to you? Secondly, and more important to them. How are you going to pay it back? The business plan, will show what your business entails. It will also show investors that you know what you are doing.

Banks want to know that they can trust you with their money and that you are a good investment. If you can't show them on paper exactly what they are investing in, how it will be profitable, and what percentage they are getting in return; then chances are that you will be left funding your own business.

So how do you write a business plan? You've never written one before. Let's begin with the most common business association in the United States of America; The Small Business Association. The SBA has been around for many years to aid beginning business get a good start on their businesses. They keep businesses accountable and a good business will help boost the local economy.

The Small Business Association is a great place to begin for the individual, small business owner hopeful, in that it has many helpful links and websites to aid you in getting started. Aside from this, their website offers a simple, yet effective way to begin your business plan. The Small Business Association website offers a template for you to follow step by step to create your business plan from inception to conception. Here it is below!

https://www.sba.gov/content/important-business-plan-tool-announcement

There are two basic classes of business plans. One is the traditional, and the other is the simple plan. The traditional is a bit longer; however, it is the one that banks are looking for if you are looking for them to invest their money with you. The latter is the simple plan.

This plan can be used if you simply want to have a straightforward way of showcasing your business and you are not in need of funding. Keep in mind, you don't have to stick to these exact formats. They are simply a guide for you to use according to the needs of your business.

At the beginning is the executive summary. The executive summary will tell your reader what your company is and why it will be successful. When in doubt, keep it simple. This section will also ask for your mission statement. You may have heard when going to interviews and seen written on their walls somewhere a poster with the business's mission and vision statement on it. To put it plainly; the mission is what the business hopes to accomplish. The reason for your company's existence if you will. While the vision statement informs the reader of how your business plans to get there.

Company Description

If you've already thought enough about your company to decide to start one, then this part should be fairly simple for your to write down. Your company's description will be to provide detailed information about your company. You're going to want to provide as much detail about the problems your business solves as possible. Don't leave any points out. Be specific, and list out the consumers, organization, or businesses your company plans to serve. You may also want to have a good idea about who your competition is.

What are the weaknesses of your competitors? Explain the competitive advantages that will make your set your business apart from the rest. .You want to have a good understanding of your industry's target market. The research that you do on your competition will show you what other businesses are doing and what their strengths are. Research to look for trends and themes. What do successful businesses do, and why? Now how can you do it better? Who are the experts on your team? Where is the location of your business? Since this is where you will get your funding, this is a good time for your company to really boast about your strengths. It's also a good idea to know your weaknesses. This way, you can focus in on them and work at strengthening them up.

This next part is very important; especially due to the class of business that you form. Will you incorporate or simply have a city business license? I strongly encourage you to consider incorporating and I'll get into the why and what that entails later in the reading. First, I'd like to get into the next part of the business plan; which is your organizational chart and management ladder.

Organization and Management

This section deals with how your will have your business set up. In other words, what will your management structure look like and how will it be organized? Who will run it? What will their title be? How many people will be in your organization? What are their roles in how the business is run? Finally, what will the legal structure be? Put simply, this is how it's formed in order to decide on how it will be taxed.

There are several types of business entity labels out there, and I will address only the most basic and broad aspects of this.

Legal Structure

The legal structure in my experience really depends on how big your company is or how big you envision it to become. The larger your business, honestly, the liable you are when things come up. When I say things come up, I mean things like lawsuites, accidents, insurance, etc. In other words, if something occurs that will cost you financially, then you don't want it to come out of your own pocket and possibly harm your family. This is what could happen if you don't incorporate.

Registering yourself as a business with the city is legally all that you need to do to get started, but then you will be responsible for all of the financial aspects of the business.

If you will be solely running the business, and you want to keep your personal assets safe from lawsuits and accidents, then I suggest incorporating as a Limited Liability Corporation or LLC.

A Limited Liability Corporation or LLC protects you from personal liability in most instances, your personal assets — like your vehicle, house, and savings accounts — won't be at risk in case your LLC faces bankruptcy or lawsuits. Profits and losses can get passed through to your personal income without facing corporate taxes. However, members of an LLC are considered self-employed and must pay self-employment tax contributions towards Medicare and Social Security.

If you are quite a bit larger of a business with say; a few thousand employees, then you may want to look at a C corporation. A corporation, sometimes called a C corp, is a legal entity that is separate from its owners. Corporations can make a profit, be taxed, and can be held legally liable. It's said that corporations offer the strongest protection to its owners from personal liability, but the cost to form a corporation is higher than other structures. Corporations also require more extensive record-keeping, operational processes, and reporting.

Unlike sole proprietors, and LLCs, corporations pay income tax on their profits. In some cases, corporate profits are taxed twice — first, when the company makes a profit, and again when dividends are paid to shareholders on their personal tax returns.

Corporations have a completely independent life separate from its shareholders. If a shareholder leaves the company or sells his or her shares, the C corp can continue doing business relatively undisturbed. On another note, corporations can raise funds through the sale of stock, which can also be a benefit in attracting employees. So if your business needs to raise money, then the C corporation might be the way to go.

There are several other classes of corporations that I can go over, I want to stick with the basics that people popularly use. Which leads me to this final one; the non profit.

The 501c (3) or non profit corporation. Non-profits are often called 501(c)(3) corporations — a reference to the section of the Internal Revenue Code that is most commonly used to grant tax-exempt status. You honestly didn't need to know that but it may come in handy one day. For now just realize that the non profit corporation is used when business serves the general public, such as a church or homeless shelter.

Nonprofit corporations are organized to do charity, education, religious, literary, or scientific work. Because their work benefits the public, non-profits can receive tax-exempt status, meaning they don't pay state or federal taxes income taxes on any profits it makes. My little disclaimer when it comes to non profits is this. Nonprofit corporations need to follow organizational rules very similar to a regular C corp. They also need to follow special rules about what they do with any profits they earn. For example, they can't distribute profits to members or political campaigns.

What Services Does Your Business Provide?

What Services Does Your Business Provide? This may be the most obvious question that anyone interested in your business will want to know, so you'd better know it. This is also why it is included in every business plan. The bank is sure going to want to know this answer, as well as your investors.

Describe what you sell or what service you offer. Explain how it benefits your customers and what the product life cycle looks like. Share your plans for intellectual property, like copyright or patent filings. If you're doing research and development for your service or product, explain it in detail. The last thing that you want is to have anyone, even remotely confused as to what you do or offer in your business of choice.

Marketing and Sales

Honestly, this is the most fun section of this informational booklet. This is how you will draw in people, in order to compel them to want to buy from you. The one question you really want to ask yourself is; "why should I buy from you"? People spend thousands of dollars to pay firms to create advertisements for their businesses, in order to make money. However, if you are very clever and saavay, then you can do this for yourself. This is where social media comes in.

Everyone uses social media; Facebook, Linkedin, Instagram, Pinterest, Twitter, to just name a few. Let's face it, if you already have a good size following, then you have your customers, already lined up to help you succeed. This is another booklet that I'll be releasing soon to help you succeed in marketing down the road.

In a nutshell, There's no single way to approach a marketing strategy. Your strategy should evolve and change to fit your unique needs. Your goal in this section is to describe how you'll attract and retain customers. You'll also describe how a sale will actually happen. You'll refer to this section later when you make financial projections, so make sure to thoroughly describe your complete marketing and sales strategies.

Funding Request

When I ask most people, why aren't they in business for themselves, one of the most common excuses is that I don't have the money. Well this is where you make your funding request to your bank or private investors. If you're asking for funding, this is where you'll outline your funding requirements. Your goal is to clearly explain how much funding you'll need over the next five years and what you'll use it for.

Specify whether you want debt or equity, the terms you'd like applied, and the length of time your request will cover. Give a detailed description of how you'll use your funds. Specify if you need funds to buy equipment or materials, pay salaries, or cover specific bills until revenue increases. Always include a description of your future strategic financial plans, like paying off debt or selling your business.

Financial Projections

Supplement your funding request with financial projections. Your goal is to convince the reader that your business is stable and will be a financial success. If your business is already established, include income statements, balance sheets, and cash flow statements for the last three to five years. If you have other collateral you could put against a loan, make sure to list it now.

Provide a prospective financial outlook for the next five to ten years. After all, you're in this for the long haul, so why not make some accountability plans to help you to be successful. Include forecasted income statements, balance sheets, cash flow statements, and capital expenditure budgets. For the first year, be even more specific and use quarterly — or even monthly — projections. Make sure to clearly explain your projections, and match them to your funding requests. If you're really clever; this is a great place to use graphs and charts to tell the financial story of your business. I didn't do this in my business plan, but every little bit helps. Pretend the bank is a classroom of middle school students. You want to keep their attention and you want to keep them interested.

Your Business Plan Appendix

This is the final section of your business plan

which provides supporting documents or other materials specifically requested. Common items to include are credit histories, resumes, product pictures, letters of reference, licenses, permits, or patents, legal documents, permits, and other contracts. I personally found this to be a bit cumbersome, but when I watched an investor flip through my business plan for the first time, I was so happy that I included it; and so were they.

Sample

I'm not going to send you off and say good luck. I've included a sample business plan below that you may use, to guide you in writing your business plan. It's very basic in format, but it has all of the elements that you will need to get your business plan going.

Thank you for loaning me your time to read this and I'm happy that you found yourself worthy to invest in.

Stefan N. Chapman,

co-founder Ever Plentiful (EP Capital),

This example business plan is provided by the Small Business Administration.

Get help starting and running your small business at SBA.gov.

WE CAN DO IT CONSULTING

BUSINESS PLAN

RON CHAMPION, OWNER

Created on September 29, 2019

Executive Summary

PRODUCT

We Can Do It Consulting provides consultation services to small- and medium-sized companies. Our services include office management and business process reengineering to improve efficiency and reduce administrative costs.

CUSTOMERS

The target audience for We Can Do It Consulting is business owners, human resources directors, program managers, presidents, or CEOs with 5 to 500 employees who want to increase productivity and reduce overhead costs. Specifically, we specialize in consulting white collar executives on office processes such as job tracking, production, getting the most out of meetings, leadership, financial or hiring best practices, and other needs relevant to potential customers who serve in a management role within small or large organizations that may be bogged down by processes, bureaucracy, or technical experts with little leadership experience.

FUTURE OF THE COMPANY

Consulting is a fast-paced, evolving industry. In response to this climate, We Can Do It Consulting will offer other services, including facilitation and requirements analysis in the future.

COMPANY DESCRIPTION

MISSION STATEMENT

To provide quality services to our clients that will help their companies prosper and grow.

PRINCIPAL MEMBERS

Rebecca Champ — owner, primary consultant

Guy Champ — business manager/sales

Sophie Roberts — account manager

LEGAL STRUCTURE

We Can Do It Consulting is an S Corporation, incorporated in Greenville, South Carolina.

MARKET RESEARCH

INDUSTRY

We Can Do It Consulting will join the office management and business process improvement consulting industry. Generally, larger consulting firms, such as KEG Consulting, work with international corporations while smaller consulting firms work with both large corporations and smaller organizations, usually closer to home. Consulting firms structured like ours also have a history of working with local, state, and federal government agencies. The consulting industry is still recovering from the economic recession. It was hit hardest in 2009 when the industry shrank by 9.1%. However, as the economy recovers, the industry is showing signs of growth. A recent study stated that operations management consulting is projected to grow by 5.1% per year for the next several years.

DETAILED DESCRIPTION OF CUSTOMERS

The target customers for We Can Do It Consulting are business owners, human resources directors, program managers, presidents or CEOs with 5 to 500 employees who want to increase productivity and reduce overhead costs. Specifically, we specialize in consulting white collar executives on office processes such as job tracking, production, getting the most out of meetings, leadership, financial or hiring best practices, and other needs relevant to potential customers who serve in a management role within small or large organizations that may be bogged down by processes, bureaucracy, or technical experts with little leadership experience. To capitalize on opportunities that are geographically close as we start and grow our business, We Can Do It Consulting will specifically target executives within companies in the manufacturing, automotive, healthcare, and defense industries. This will allow us to take advantage of the company's close proximity to hospitals (one of the largest employers in the region), automobile and vehicle parts factories, and government contractors supporting the nearby former Air Force base, now an aviation technology center.

COMPANY ADVANTAGES

Because We Can Do It Consulting provides services, as opposed to a product, our advantages are only as strong as our consultants. Aside from ensuring our team is flexible, fast, can provide expert advice and can work on short deadlines, we will take the following steps to support consulting services:

- Maintain only PMP-certified project managers
- Ensure account team members use our proprietary planning and reporting process to stay in touch with customers and keep them updated on projects
- Provide public speaking training for all consultants
- Develop close relationships with subcontractors who can support us in areas such as graphic design, to ensure materials and presentations are always clear and maintain a consistent brand

- All our staff members have at least a four-year degree, with 20% having an advanced degree
- We are a virtual company without a lot of overhead costs or strict corporate rules, which saves time, money and creates a flexible workplace for getting things done

REGULATIONS

We Can Do It Consulting must meet all Federal and state regulations concerning business consulting. Specifically, Code of Federal Regulations in Title 64, Parts 8753 and 4689.62, 65, and 74 and Title 86.7 of the Code of South Carolina.

SERVICE LINE

PRODUCT/ SERVICE

Services Include:
- Business Process Reengineering Analysis
- Office Management Analysis
- On-Site Office Management Services
- Business Process Reengineering Facilitation
- Analytics
- Change Management
- Customer Relationship Management
- Financial Performance
- Operations Improvement
- Risk Management

PRICING STRUCTURE

We Can Do It Consulting will offer its services at an hourly rate using the following labor categories and rates:

- Principal, $150
- Account Executive, $140
- Project Manager, $135
- Project Coordinator, $100
- Business Analyst, $90
- Process Analyst, $90
- Financial Analyst, $85
- Technologist, $75

PRODUCT LIFECYCLE

All services are ready to be offered to clients, pending approval of contracts.

INTELLECTUAL PROPERTY RIGHTS

We Can Do It Consulting is a trademarked name in the state of South Carolina, and we have filed for protection of our proprietary processes and other intellectual property, such as our logo. We have also registered our domain name and parked relevant social media accounts for future use and to prevent the likelihood of someone impersonating one of our consultants.

RESEARCH AND DEVELOPMENT

The company is planning to conduct the following research and development:

- Create a custom technology solution for manufacturers of vehicles such as automobiles or airplanes that helps better track each manufactured piece and its status in the assembly process

- Determine the need for additional consulting services within our market related to tying improved processes to opportunities for increased sales and promotion to potential customers

- Find trends in software solutions that may provide potentially competitive automated services in order to ensure We Can Do It Consulting continues to carefully carve its niche in the marketplace

MARKETING & SALES

GROWTH STRATEGY

To grow the company, We Can Do It Consulting will do the following:

- Network at manufacturing, automobile industry, and healthcare conferences
- Establish a company website that contains engaging multimedia content about our services
- As the business grows, advertise in publications that reach our target industries

COMMUNICATE WITH THE CUSTOMER

We Can Do It Consulting will communicate with its customers by:

- Meeting with local managers within targeted companies
- Using social media such as Twitter, YouTube, Facebook, and LinkedIn
- Providing contact information on the company website

HOW TO SELL

Currently, the only person in charge of sales for We Can Do It Consulting is the business manager, Guy Champ. As profits increase, We Can Do It will look to add an employee to assist with account management/coordination. This individual will also provide company social media and online marketing support. The company will increase awareness to our targeted customers through online advertising, proactive public relations campaigns, and attending trade shows.

www.ingramcontent.com/pod-product-compliance
Lightning Source LLC
Chambersburg PA
CBHW070842220526
45466CB00002B/856